JAKE'S GOLDEN HANDBOOK

Jake's Gold Finding Tips for Kids

Robin Adolphs   Jenny James

BUTTERNUT

Published by Butternut Books 2017

Copyright © 2017 Robin Adolphs

All rights reserved. No part of this publication may be reproduced, stored in a retrieval system, or transmitted in any form or by any means, electronic, mechanical, photocopying, recording or otherwise, without the prior written permission from the publisher.

A catalogue record for this book is available from the National Library of Australia.

Grandpa's Gold illustrations by Arthur Filloy
Illustrations by Jenny James

Book cover design and formatting services by BookCoverCafe.com

www.RobinAdolphs.com

ISBN:
978-0-9942121-8-4 (pbk)
978-0-9942121-9-1 (e-bk)

Saguaros, Nurse Trees, Packrats and Infection

I've lived a long time and I've kept my eyes open. I've seen that the story of a saguaro and its nurse tree doesn't always end the same way. Remember the cholla and the packrats?

If there's enough rain so the cholla can produce lots of buds, there will be lots of packrat food. And soon there will be many packrats. One of the packrats might make a nest under the nurse tree while the tree is still fairly healthy. And the packrat might climb the nurse tree, run out on a branch that touches the saguaro, and eat a hole in the cactus! Or it might expand a hole that was started by a woodpecker.

If a packrat climbs out on a limb that touches the saguaro, it can chew a hole in the cactus.

If a packrat chews a hole in the saguaro, fruit flies and other insects might come to get the exposed moisture. And the insects may bring *bacteria* that infect the saguaro and might even kill it. The dead cactus will eventually fall over, and you may see its skeleton next to the surviving nurse tree.

If the wound made by the packrat gets infected, the infection can kill the saguaro. The cactus falls over and rots, leaving only its skeleton.

Jackrabbits, Saguaros and Rain

After a period of wet weather, there are many tender green plants, and the jackrabbits have plenty to eat. They have more babies, and the jackrabbit population increases. Adult males become *territorial.* That means they protect the space they need to find food and raise their family. Sometimes this protection includes fighting other jackrabbits to defend territory.

More often the jackrabbits just mark their territory by digging shallow pits, especially along ridges. They pee and poop into these pits. Each male might dig several pits, spaced out to mark his territory.

The marked pits are a way of saying "This space is taken. The plants around here are mine to eat. Go find someplace else."

A jackrabbit may "box" with another to defend his territory.

When there are many jackrabbits, the adult males dig shallow pits.

Time goes by, and the desert dries out again. Since there's not much rain, the plants don't grow much. There are many jackrabbits still alive from the wetter times, but now there's a limited supply of food. When the hungry jackrabbits get desperate for food and water, they eat young saguaros. They chew as high up as they can reach.

If the jackrabbits leave enough of the green living part of the saguaro still connected to its roots, the saguaro might be able to keep growing. But sometimes the connection is completely broken. Water can't get from the roots to the green growing parts of the saguaro, and food made by the green parts can't reach the roots. The saguaro dies.

In the dry times, without much to eat, the jackrabbits don't live as long, and they have fewer babies. But remember the pits the adult males dug and marked with pee and poo when there were many more jackrabbits? Well, over time, the wind blows the seeds of many desert plants into those pits.

When the rains finally return, the shallow pits catch the water. Now we have fertilizer, seeds, and water in the pits, all together. So what do you think happens next?

The wind blows seeds into the jackrabbit pits.

If you look closely, you can see that this saguaro has a living green strip that connects the living top of the cactus with the roots.

This saguaro has died because no connection remained between the roots and the top of the plant.

Rainwater has collected in this pit.

That's right! The seeds take root and grow, making new patches of tender green plants. And once a patch is started, it can grow bigger, beyond the pit.

Patches of vegetation can get a start in jackrabbit pits.

These patches of plants are good for me, because there's lots of food for a desert tortoise in each plant cluster. By starting these patches, the jackrabbit helps make food for other animals. This and many other animal-and-plant interactions are important to the desert *ecosystem* — all the plants and animals you see when you visit us in El Pinacate.

Patches of vegetation grow beyond the jackrabbit pits where they started.

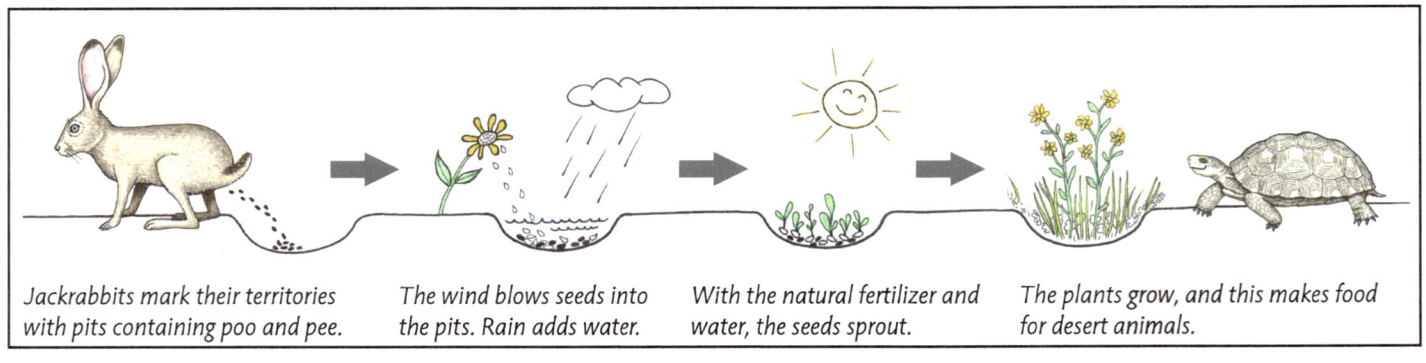

Jackrabbits mark their territories with pits containing poo and pee.

The wind blows seeds into the pits. Rain adds water.

With the natural fertilizer and water, the seeds sprout.

The plants grow, and this makes food for desert animals.

Now you know something about my desert home in El Pinacate:

• *Rain* is very important in this desert. With more rain, the *chollas* will grow more buds. Also, more tender green plants will sprout and grow. *page 4*

• The number of cholla buds blowing around the desert determines how many buds there are for *packrats* — and for me — and how many new cholla plants will grow. *page 7*

• The number of chollas determines how many young *ocotillo* plants are protected from sun and cold and from being eaten by *black-tailed jackrabbits* and other animals. *page 14*

• The sprouting and growth of the many other kinds of plants brings food for the black-tailed jackrabbit to eat. And since the rain allows the plants to grow, it's the rainfall that determines how many jackrabbits there will be. *page 23*

• The number of jackrabbits affects how many *pits* they make to mark their territories, and how many *patches* of new plants will grow from the pits when the rain comes. *page 26*

As you explore, I hope you can see the desert through my eyes:

• When you see an ocotillo with many spreading branches, think of the cholla that protected it when it was small. If you see a tall, straight ocotillo, think of the jackrabbit that nibbled on its young branches. *page 8*

• When you see a *saguaro* standing tall and alone, know that once a *nurse tree* might have protected it. *page 17*

• If you see a saguaro skeleton lying on the ground, maybe it's because a packrat chewed a hole in the cactus and an infection set in. *page 21*

• If you see a saguaro that has been chewed as high up as a jackrabbit can reach, understand that weather and changes in the jackrabbit population led to a shortage of plants. The jackrabbits were very hungry. *page 24*

Please visit El Pinacate often. Look around. There's much more to learn here. If you're very lucky, you might see a desert tortoise. We plan to be here awhile.

About the Author

Renaldo, a Sonoran desert tortoise, lives on the top of Mount Salvatierra, where he has a good view of the changes and processes that happen in his El Pinacate desert ecosystem over several decades. Lacking fingers, a camera and a computer, he recruited **Paul Dayton,** a visiting biologist, to tell his story.

For all kids who love adventures

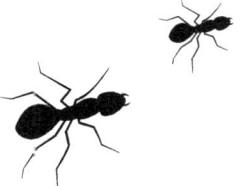

Contents

About Jake 1

Jake's Tips for Kids 2

    Before you start 2

    You need to learn 2

    How do you find the areas? 3

    What to look for 3

    Some DON'TS! 3

    The 3 Golden Rules 4

    Don't be fooled! 4

Panning for Gold 5

Detecting for Gold 6

    What you'll need 6

        Parts of the Detector 6

    What you do 7

        Before you start using a detector make sure 7

        When you are ready to start 7

For BOTH panning and detecting you'll also need 9

And if you're camping in the bush you'll also need 10

Interviews

    Karl 11

    Barry and Olga 14

    'Mulga' Bill. 17

    Joan 19

A picture of the real life Jake 21

Riddle Answers 21

Gold Terms and Meanings 22

Other Books by Robin 26

About Jake

Hi, I'm Jake. I was three years old when I first went with my grandparents to Clermont in Central Queensland. I was there again when I was seven and that's when I found my first piece of gold.

We stayed in the Clermont Caravan Park and I got to meet all the people there. I loved the bush and looking for gold. It was a great experience and I'm happy to share some of the things I learned with you.

All the people in this book I have met. They're all great people. I hope you have the chance to someday go into the Australian bush. Here are some tips for you, just in case you one day go camping in the bush and look for gold.

What does a gold prospector like to eat?

Answer page 21

Jake's Tips for Kids

If you'd like to go looking for gold, here are some of the things you need to do.

Before you start...

* Make sure you and an adult have talked to someone who knows the area you want to go to.

* Tell someone where you'll be going and how long you will be away, in case you get lost or have an accident.

compass

walkie-talkie

You need to learn...

* To be prepared.

* How to use a GPS, a compass or the position of the sun to find your way in the bush in case you get separated from an adult.

* To use a walkie-talkie.

* About the animals, reptiles and insects in the region.

* How to use a detector or gold pan properly.

* Always go with an adult and never, ever go on your own!

How do you find the areas?

An adult will probably take you to areas where gold has been found in the past.

When you get there, look for signs that gold was there.

What to look for

* Quartz rock
* Ironstone
* Old diggings
* Old-timer camps
* Old rubbish like tobacco tins, nails, horseshoes, buttons (these will all probably be rusty)

Some DON'TS!

* Never step over a fallen log without looking first. There might be a snake lying on the other side.
* Walk, don't run. You could trip over fallen branches or run into a spider's web.

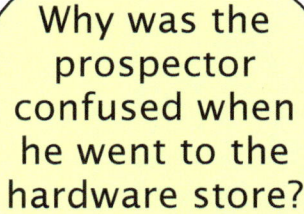

Why was the prospector confused when he went to the hardware store?

Answer page 21

Looking for gold is great fun. Happy hunting, but remember...

The 3 Golden Rules

1. Fill in any holes you dig.
2. Take your rubbish with you when you leave.
3. Leave the bush the way you found it!

Don't be fooled!

Fool's gold looks like gold but is really a mineral called iron pyrite. It became known as fool's gold because early prospectors were fooled by its colour.

Can you change FOOL into GOLD in three steps?

Answer page 21

fool's gold (iron pyrite)   real gold nugget!

Panning for Gold

Ridges in the pan catch the fine gold.

gold pan

What you'll need

* A gold pan
* Water
* Stones, sand or dirt from the edge of a creek
* AN ADULT!

What you do

1. Scoop the stones and sand into your pan.
2. Gently sink the pan into the water and slosh it around, from side to side and in a circular motion.
3. Keep swirling the mixture (called a slurry) of stone, sand and water around, tipping the edge of the pan into the water to let the small stones and soil wash out.
4. The gold will settle at the bottom of the pan as it is heavy.

* You can pick out the bigger stones. Just make sure you're not throwing away any gold!

Where do prospectors keep their gold?

Answer page 21

Detecting for Gold

What you'll need

* A detector
* A charged battery and headphones
* A pick
* AN ADULT!

pick with a flat end and a pointed end

Parts of the Detector

Minelab GPX 5000 gold detector   More information at www.minelab.com
Special thanks to Minelab for the image

What you do

Before you start using a detector make sure...

* It's tuned in and working. Throw a coin on the ground and wave the detector over it. If it's working you'll hear it!

* You have all the attachments you need like coils and tape in case something comes loose.

* The batteries are charged.

* You have a plastic bag to cover the detector in case it rains. Don't let it get wet.

Where can a prospector always find gold?

Answer page 21

When you are ready to start...

1. Switch on the metal detector.

2. Lift it up and down a couple of times to see if it's properly tuned. It will be noisy at first but it will fade to a quiet humming sound.

3. Slowly walk along swinging the detector slowly from side to side, very close to the ground.

4. If you get a signal, stop walking and wave the detector over the spot from side to side until you think you've found the exact spot.

5. Scrape away the leaves and stones with your boot or the side of your pick. Wave the detector over the spot again to see if the metal is still in the ground or you've scraped it out.

6. Keep picking, scraping and listening until the sound is no longer coming from the hole but is out in one of the heaps you've made.

7. Then it's down on your hands and knees. Put your detector on the ground. Pick up handfuls of dirt and stones where you think the metal is and wave your fist back and forth over the detector coil. Keep doing this until the detector makes a noise. That means you're holding metal (hopefully gold) in your hand.

8. Transfer some of the dirt and stones to your other hand so you have piles in both hands. Run your hands over the detector coil again and throw away the pile that is silent. Keep doing this until all you have in your hand is the gold.

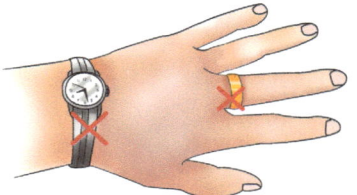

Hint: Don't wear a watch or ring when you have your hands near the detector, as they will give a signal.

9. Remember to fill in the hole before you leave.

Knock knock
Who's there?
Doug
Doug who?

Doug a hole and found a gold nugget.

For BOTH panning and detecting you'll also need...

* Protective clothing
* Lots of water to drink
* Food
* Sunscreen
* Insect spray
* A two-way walkie-talkie is a good idea too!
* GPS or compass and a map of the area
* First aid kit
* A licence (for gold mining), if you are going into state forests

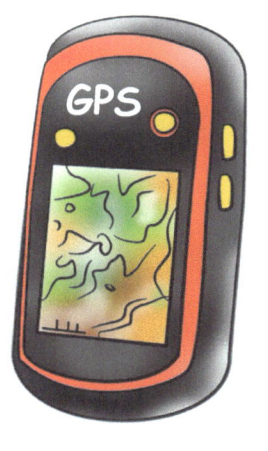

walkie-talkie

And if you're camping in the bush you'll also need...

- Shelter, a tent is good
- Sleeping bags
- Battery operated light (a torch)
- Extra batteries
- Shovel to dig a hole
- Extra food and water
- A mobile phone is good but sometimes you can't get reception in the bush
- A battery operated radio is also good for weather reports

Jake Interviews Real Life Prospectors!

Karl

My first interview is with my grandpa, Karl. He's the grandpa in *Grandpa's Gold*. He taught me just about everything I know about looking for gold.

How long have you been detecting for gold?
I've been detecting for gold for 17 years.

Where have you been detecting?
I go to places where the old-timers found gold about 130 years ago. You can get maps of gold areas from the Mines Department. I've detected in Queensland, Victoria, New South Wales and Western Australia.

What do you like about detecting?
I love the peace and quiet of the bush and being surrounded by nature. It's healthy walking around the bush and you get lots of exercise. You have to look out for snakes though.

It's a great feeling when you find gold. Once you find gold you want to keep finding it. You get gold fever which means you don't want to stop. Gold is worth a lot of money.

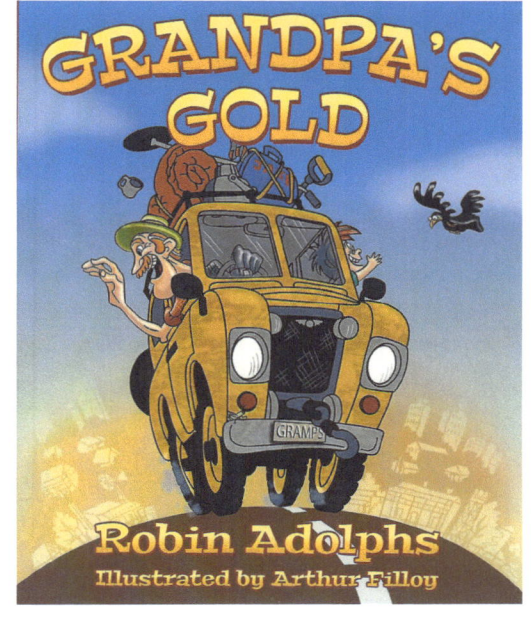

These are some of the places in Australia my grandpa Karl and his friends have been to look for gold.

There are many other places in Australia where gold can be found.

What's the funniest thing that ever happened to you when you were looking for gold?
It didn't happen to me but to my wife. It was pretty funny though. We drove into the bush and set up camp one day.

I set off with my detector and my wife stayed near the car. Suddenly she heard loud mooing. On the other side of the track were a big black bull and ten cows. The bull was getting madder and madder because the cows kept walking away from him.

He kept mooing and mooing, getting louder and louder but the cows ignored him and walked off. Suddenly the bull turned his head and saw my wife. Well, she got a bit nervous as she didn't want the bull coming after her. So she got up and opened all the car doors ready to jump in the nearest one in case the bull came charging.

After a while of staring at one another, the bull lost interest and left. It was pretty funny to get back to the car and see my wife peeking around the side of the car.

Do you have any tips for kids?
Look for creeks where there are old-timer diggings. These are heaps of soil, also called throw-outs or mullock heaps, that the old-timers dug out of the creek. They wanted to get under the soil and stones on top of the creek bed to the layer below called the wash. The gold is heavy and is usually under the wash. Always go detecting with an adult.

Knock knock
Who's there?
Phil
Phil who?
Phil in the hole so I don't step in it and break my leg!

Barry and Olga

Barry and Olga owned the Gold Detector Shop in Clermont and loved detecting together. Olga is a happy and generous lady and Barry taught me lots of things about gold. I did this interview with Olga, as sadly Barry died in 2010.

How long have you been detecting for gold?
We've been detecting for gold since the 1990's.

Where have you been detecting?
Barry's dad was the tour guide at the Long Tunnel Gold Mine at Walhalla, in Victoria. We panned and detected there, then we went to the Clermont goldfields for a one month holiday and we're still here!

What do you like about detecting?

We loved going out in the bush with the birds, dingoes, emus, echidnas and cattle. It's so peaceful away from the noise and bustle of town life.

When we owned the Gold Detector Shop we met lots of different people from all over the world who were looking for adventure and new exciting things to do.

We loved the school excursions. Barry used to dress up and show the school kids how to use a detector and how to pan for gold.

Finding gold is a bonus! When you find a piece of gold you want to keep on looking for more. It's a bit like fishing, you don't know if you're going to catch anything but when you do, it's GOLD FEVER!

What's the funniest thing that ever happened to you when you were looking for gold?

We were detecting on the banks of a dry river bed. There was a fallen tree ahead and as I (Olga) approached the tree I heard a loud squeal. I got such a fright I jumped in the air and suddenly there was a black feral pig. He jumped up and took off. I think I woke him up. I was scared stiff and I think the pig was too!

Do you have any tips for kids?
Lots! Cover up. Have good shoes, a good hat, long sleeves and pants and sunscreen. Watch out for snakes. Carry a water bottle and a snack. If you can, have a lesson on how to use a detector. That's great!

Look for quartz, ironstone and turkey bushes. They're signs that gold might be there. Mark out an area and make a grid, follow the lines and work over the area slowly.

A map of Australia that Olga made from gold nuggets found near Clermont.

What do gold prospectors and rabbits have in common?

Answer page 21

'Mulga' Bill

'Mulga' is Bill's nickname but it suits him. He's one of my grandpa's best mates. He's a great bushman and knows so much about the bush he could probably write his own book about it.

How long have you been detecting for gold?
I've been detecting for gold since 1995. When I was a boy my dad took me panning and specking for gold. My grand-dad and great uncle panned and specked for gold too. I guess it's in the blood.

Where have you been detecting?
Dad took me specking near Bendigo in Victoria. I've detected for gold in the Rockhampton area and at Cloncurry in Queensland and the Central West of Queensland. I've also been to Western Australia.

What do you like about detecting?
I like the quietness, it's very relaxing. Occasionally I like the company of other prospectors.

It's unreal when you find something that's been in the ground for millions of years and no-one's ever found it before. It always gives you a buzz when you find even the smallest piece of gold. It's a challenge.

What's the funniest thing that ever happened to you when you were looking for gold?
My mate Karl and I were in Western Australia. Karl was about 200 metres away from me. Suddenly I saw a swarm of bees heading straight for Karl. The swarm was almost one metre thick and about seven metres long. In other words it was huge. There must have been a thousand bees and Karl was right in their path. He had his headphones on and was looking at the ground so he didn't see or hear them.

I started jumping and waving and hollering at him to warn him. Finally he saw me and realised what was happening. He bit the dust and lay flat on the ground just as the swarm flew right over the top of him.

It was a really dangerous situation but I couldn't stop laughing. He looked so funny sprawled flat out on the ground like a dead tree. At the time it wasn't funny, but afterwards when we weren't so shocked we had a good laugh. We both looked pretty funny that day.

Do you have any tips for kids?
Always learn from one of the old boys. They've had lots of experience. Be prepared for anything.

Wherever you're going, go with someone who knows the area. Never go alone. Carry a GPS or compass and lots of water.

Joan

Joan is a legend! She can talk to you about anything at all and is always interested in other people. She's one of the most interesting people I have met.

How long have you been detecting for gold?
About 20 years.

Where have you been detecting?
I started panning at Hill End out of Bathurst, 20 years ago. After that I went to Tarnagulla in the Golden Triangle area of Victoria and then on to Clermont. I've been here 14 years and I'm still looking for gold. It's harder to find now and you can search all day sometimes and not find any.

What do you like about detecting?
Lots of things. Gold is valuable but that's not the main reason why I go prospecting. I love being in the bush. I love nature and love to see the animals and birds. It's very relaxing. Being with nature gives me strength and makes me feel at peace.

I meet lots of people in bush towns and I talk to them about prospecting. It has helped me touch other people's lives. I have learnt from all the people I've met and shared knowledge with them.

What's the funniest thing that ever happened to you when you were looking for gold?
Lots of funny things have happened to me. One time I was digging for gold and heard a 'woomp, woomp' noise. I looked up and there were three emus looking at me. I'm sure they were talking to each other saying, 'What's she doing there?'

Once I was in the bush walking and thinking. My pick was at my side, hanging from my belt. All of a sudden the pick went between my legs and tripped me over. As I started to fall, my hat flew off and I fell on my pick. Ouch! Luckily I didn't break anything.

Another time I saw a big black-headed python on the road and turned the car around to have another look. He didn't appreciate this and started hissing at me. He left but it was funny. I'd just been told off by a snake!

black-headed python

Do you have any tips for kids?
When you're detecting for gold, listen for its sound. Keep digging as long as you can hear the sound. It can be on the surface but it could also be deep down.

When you find gold, you will feel full of energy and excited.

Here's a picture of me!

The real life Jake

Riddle Answers

* What does a gold prospector like to eat? *Nuggets*

* Why was the prospector confused when he went to the hardware store?
  He asked for a shovel and they told him to take his pick.

* Change FOOL to GOLD in three steps.
  FOOL → FOOD → GOOD → GOLD

* Where do prospectors keep their gold? *In the river bank*

* Where can a prospector always find gold? *In the dictionary*

* What do gold prospectors and rabbits have in common?
  They both like carats/carrots

Gold Terms and Meanings

Batteries	➤ Used to power detectors and torches
Bush	➤ Australian country area
Camp	➤ Temporary place to eat and sleep
Carat	➤ Measure of purity of gold - pure gold is 24 carats
Coil	➤ Disc on the bottom of a detector
Compass	➤ Direction finding device
Creek	➤ Small water course
Crystal Gold	➤ Rare type of gold that looks like crystals
Detecting	➤ Using a detector

Detector	➤ Modern tool for finding gold under the ground
Detectorist	➤ A person who uses a detector
Digger	➤ A name given to a prospector in the early days
Diggings	➤ Large holes dug by early prospectors

Dry Blower	➢ Machine to separate the gold from soil and rocks by blowing
Fines	➢ Very fine, powdery gold, often found by panning
Fool's Gold	➢ A mineral called iron pyrite sometimes mistaken for gold
Fossicker	➢ A person who tries to find gold, precious metals or gems
Fossicking	➢ Looking for gold, precious metals or gems
Gold	➢ Precious yellow metal
Gold Bottle	➢ Small bottle to store nuggets in
Gram	➢ Gold measurement - 31.1 grams in a Troy ounce
Ground Noise	➢ Noises from the ground heard through a detector
GPS	➢ Global Positioning System device
Gully	➢ Land formation between two slopes
Headphones	➢ Used with a detector to hear ground noises
Ironstone	➢ Dark rock containing iron (a mineral)
Licence	➢ Permit to fossick on government land

Metal	➤ Found in the ground e.g. gold, silver and copper - also can come from mineral ore after mining
Mineral	➤ Rocks contain minerals - if there are large amounts of useful minerals in the rocks, it is called ore and it can be mined
Mines	➤ Open or underground diggings
Mullock Heaps	➤ Heaps of dirt thrown from diggings
Nugget	➤ A chunk of gold

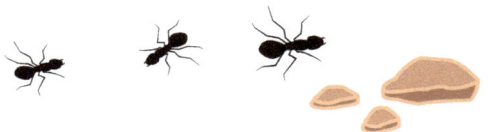

Old-timer	➤ A fossicker from the early days
Overburden	➤ Large heaps of soil from large mines

Pan	➤ A flat dish used to pan for gold
Panning	➤ The act of looking for gold using a pan
Pick	➤ A tool to dig gold nuggets out of the ground
Prospector	➤ A person who explores areas looking for gold, precious metals or gems
Quartz	➤ A whitish rock that gold is sometimes attached to

Scales	➢ Used for weighing gold nuggets and fines
Shaft (1)	➢ Long rod that is part of the detector
Shaft (2)	➢ Tunnel dug into the ground
Shale	➢ Rock that forms in flat layers
Shovel	➢ Used for digging holes
Sluice Box	➢ Box used for separating gold from soil from the creek
Slurry	➢ A mixture of stones, sand, dirt and water
Specimen	➢ Gold attached to other rocks e.g. quartz
Specking	➢ Looking for gold with your eyes on the ground surface
Throw-outs	➢ Soil thrown out of creeks or diggings
Troy Ounce	➢ Gold measurement - 31.1 grams
Turkey Bush	➢ 1 to 2 metre tall bush with thin branches and small narrow leaves
Walkie-Talkie	➢ A two-way radio
Wash	➢ Layer of fine stones and dirt under the top layer of soil
Wet Plant	➢ Machine to separate gold from soil using water

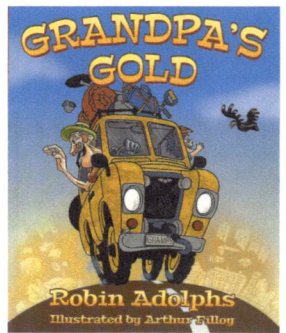  

Other Books by Robin

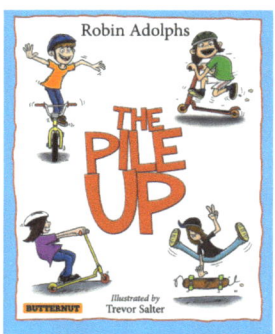  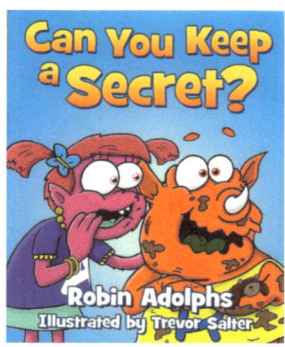

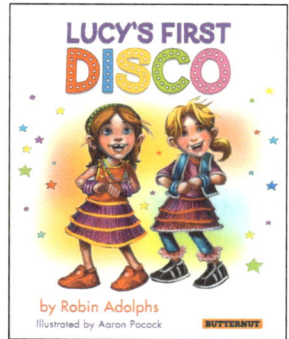 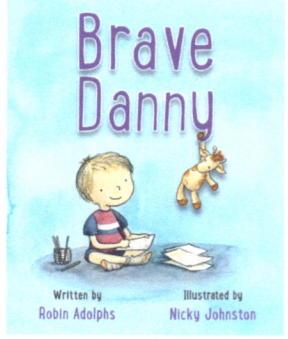

Available at Amazon

For more free activities and puzzles go to

RobinAdolphs.com

www.ingramcontent.com/pod-product-compliance
Lightning Source LLC
Chambersburg PA
CBHW041126300426
44113CB00002B/73